A CANDLE ON FIRE

A POTPOURRI OF POEMS

A CANDLE ON FIRE

A POTPOURRI OF POEMS

EDDIE MORALES

A CANDLE ON FIRE

A POTPOURRI OF POEMS

Copyright © 2012 by EDDIE MORALES

All rights reserved. No part of this book may be reproduced or transmitted in any form or by any means without written permission of the author.

ISBN 9781938094026

THIS BOOK IS DEDICATED

To my children, Veronica, Chloe, and Peter

To my grandchildren, E.J., Gabriel, and Ileana

Acknowledgments

To all who know me:

In my solitude, I find myself,

In your friendship, well I lose myself.

OTHER BOOKS YOU MAY ENJOY

A Reason for Rhyme

The Suicide Sonnets

Count Edweird Lefang's Rhymin' Halloween

Foreword

When reading a poem, or when listening to someone reciting a poem, I first and foremost pay attention to the language. It is the words that are important. What words did you select in putting your poem together? Did you use syntax, tone, imagery, metaphor, or other parts of speech to enhance your poem? All of these things, and more, are part of the language of poetry.

Firstly, let me ask a question: *Se avete intenzione di trasferirsi in un altro paese, cosa si deve fare prima di andare lì?* I'm sorry. You say you don't understand Italian. *Mama mia!* Well, let me rephrase: *Si se va a mudar a un país extranjero, ¿qué debe hacer en primer lugar para poder sobrevivir allí?* What's that you say? *Madre sagrada!* You don't understand Spanish. Okay, let me ask the question still another way: *Si vous allez déménager dans un autre pays, ce qui devrait vous faire avant de vous y allez?* What's that you say? *Sacre bleu!* You don't understand French either. Okay then, how about this: If you plan to live in a foreign country, what should you do first in order to survive there? For me the answer is simple. One should first learn the language.

It is no different with poetry. Poetry has a language of its own, and it is a language that exists within your own, primary language; and it takes that primary language and fine tunes its words in such a manner, that with a fraction of all the words you can possibly use, you say it all, and sometimes, more.

Ah yes! There it is! Poetry is the language within its primary language which becomes more than the primary language, and elevates itself to the highest degree. Isn't that a wonderful paradox? After all, how can you take a small portion of an entire vocabulary, and create a language greater than its parent language?

Poetry is also a language which utilizes all of the elements of prose, with the added bonus, if you dare, of being able to add uniqueness to your poem through the use of rhyme. These elements are condiments on the spice rack of poetry, and like a master chef selecting ingredients and spices for a *pièce de résistance*, an *obra maestra*, an *opera d'arte*, you, as a poet, must learn all you can about poetry, and use all its elements, its vocabulary, to create your own poetic masterpiece.

I feel that the more I learn about poetry, the more I realize how little I know, and therefore, I am always in pursuit of more knowledge in regards to this highest form of writing, so I can understand it, so I can speak it well, so I can converse with it, so words in practice are words well spent, and hopefully, one day, I can master as many of, if not all, the elements of writing I have at my disposal. So, in parting, permit me one last question, in plain English: How can you write your best poetry if you don't first learn the language? Is poetry awesome, or what? I'm sorry, that's two questions.

Table of Contents

LOVE AND BEAUTY 1

    A Kiss to Remember 3

    A Mortal Love 4

    A New Door Opens 5

    Beauty 6

    Beyond the Exotic Dance 7

    Blinding Light 8

    Butterfly Dancing 9

    By Candlelight 10

    Candlelit Bedroom 11

    Cobalt Blue 13

    Dilemma 14

    Eyes I Seek 15

    Faith 16

    Flawless Love 17

    Free Fall 18

    Hail, Woman 19

    Half A Love 20

    If You Were To Fall In Love With Me 21

In Your Absence 23

I Roamed the Roads 24

It Matters Not 25

Juxtaposition 26

Love and Honey 27

Mugunghwa 28

My Little Smile 31

Next Chapter 32

Nightingale 33

Our Silhouettes 34

Silent Agony 35

Snow on Christmas Eve 36

Sometimes Love 37

The Flame 38

Transfiguration 39

Unanswered Questions 40

Wasted Nights 41

What I Have Learned 42

Wild Orchid 43

When Love Rests 45

Yours is the Face 46

TETRADS OF SONNETS 47

Tetrad I: Passion, Sonnet I 49

Tetrad I: Passion, Sonnet II 50

Tetrad I: Passion, Sonnet III 51

Tetrad I: Passion, Sonnet IV 52

Tetrad II: Hands, Sonnet I 53

Tetrad II: Hands, Sonnet II 54

Tetrad II: Hands, Sonnet III 55

Tetrad II: Hands, Sonnet IV 56

Tetrad III: My Obsession with Poetry, Sonnet I 57

Tetrad III: My Obsession with Poetry, Sonnet II 58

Tetrad III: My Obsession with Poetry, Sonnet III 59

Tetrad III: My Obsession with Poetry, Sonnet IV 60

SLAMMIN' AWAY 61

Poetry Slams 63

Bang! 65

Cool Cat 68

Perfect Universe 70

Litany of Clichés 72

Misdirection 77

The Challenge 79

The Hanging Limerick 81

    The Hanging Limerick One 83

    The Hanging Limerick Two 83

    The Hanging Limerick Three 83

    The Hanging Limerick Four 84

    The Hanging Limerick Five 84

    The Hanging Limerick Six 84

    Sixty-Nine 85

    Sixty-Nine II 85

    Sixty-Nine III 85

    The Virgin Juanita 86

    Hot Sally Decatur 86

    A Lady and a Scamp 86

    Touchy Feely Harry 87

    Kick the Bucket 87

    The Tenor Maguire 87

HODGE PODGE 89

    Back When 91

    Die! Bitch! Die! 92

    Diver Feared Drowned 93

    In Retrospect 94

My Paradox 95

Ode to Perseverance 96

Rhyme at First Hearing 97

Two Ravens at War 98

MY SENTIMENTS EXACTLY 99

A Reason for Rhyme 101

Though I'm Forgotten 103

When My Pen Runs Out of Ink 104

LOVE AND BEAUTY

A CANDLE ON FIRE

A Kiss to Remember

Give me a kiss I'll remember forever.
Even if you don't love me, I'll treasure it most
When I think of our lips—in this ancient endeavor!
In the middle of winter, when my fire is lost.

Even if you don't love me, I'll treasure it most
When I walk in the rain, or in fresh fallen snow.
In the middle of winter, when my fire is lost,
I'll close my cold eyes to dream as I go.

When I walk in the rain, or in fresh fallen snow,
The touch of your lips will warm my poor soul.
I'll close my cold eyes to dream—and go!
To the summer when our lips lived a life whole.

The touch of your lips will warm my poor soul
In times when my mind is bound to recall—
The summer when two lips lived a life whole.
It is the summer engraved in the heart of the fall!

In times when my mind is bound to recall,
This is my memory—more precious than gold!
It is the Summer engraved in the heart of the Fall,
The fire which burns wholly when winters are cold.

This is my memory—more precious than gold!
I'll think of it often and know it is good.
Burn this fire wholly!—when winters are cold.
Oh, if only you could—if only you would.

I'll think of it often and know it is good,
Of our lips locked before in this ancient endeavor.
Oh! If only you could! Oh yes, if only you would
Give me a kiss . . . I'll remember, forever.

A Mortal Love

No Venus do I favor for my love.

All plinths are clouds,
and Icarus knew late
the heavy humor of a man far above
this fragile world where
fluid wings tempt Fate.

On earthly soil my lady I await,
where passion's eyes entreat
the lips to meet
in whispered songs of
mortal love
that wake the nature of the flesh—
so frail and sweet!

And we will dance "above" the
gods beneath her feet.

A New Door Opens

Love's not denied—when purely driven,
But falsely given draws contempt.
Attempt to pass beyond the wake—
Retake the love to mend the break!
Re-define your own cognition, to fruition,
For no fate is truly sealed . . . none to fell a hope;
For every Phoenix takes the stroke,
And dares invoke the spark, the flame,
To laud its fiery fame,
Rising up in recognition
Of a spiritual connection,
Always dauntless, never tame!

Beauty

When you are beautiful,
People look at the outside of you.

When your beauty diminishes,
They look for your beauty inside.

External beauty fades quickly,
So make sure you are more beautiful
Inside than out.

This way, you are beautiful forever.

Beyond the Exotic Dance

Miss Ocean undulates upon the stage,
Without the moon, or benefit of sun;
Yet stars dance on her never tiring age,
And sun is brought to each whose day is done.
No promises are made to those who dream
Of bathing in her crashing tides of sin,
But minds do wander, for a ray, a beam,
To keep their rushing rivers rushing in.
The wavelets call the sailors out to sea,
Where some may grasp the beauty of her waves;
But most will stand on dry reality,
Content, or discontent, with land for graves.
I'll drown in Ocean's depths, un-cleansed, I know,
But that is where her filthy waters flow.

Blinding Light

Reveal your thoughts to me my blushing Rose.
What jealousy conspires to lose your face?
Why, Lily, seek to be a Moon, morose,
When being is eclipsed by greater Grace?
Why, Sun, are your rays so melancholy?
My Stars, what makes a radiant Orchid cry?
She well may be the fire who burns wholly
The enamored heart, and catches the eye!
It doesn't matter, fickle Destiny,
These vain attempts to bring my pasture gloom,
Because you know I love her, and you see,
The Daisies are no lesser for their bloom.
The Tulips bless wherever they may grow,
And bless the woman whom I've grown to know.

EDDIE MORALES

Butterfly Dancing

My wide-eyed child and I know of colorful things
that dip and skim over summer hills and meadows,
of fancy freedom held aloft by wispy wings,
of frail, orange petals edged in ebon shadows.

From grassy beds, between oaks and weeping willows,
my little garden walker and I greet the sky—
an azure floor sprinkled with fluffy white pillows,
all spot-lit by the yellow ball squinting the eye.

And the dance commences—a Monarch's pirouette!
Then a plié and rise on the breath of the breeze!
How my wide-eyed child laughs at the King's minuet
while I smile at my heart soaring over the trees.

My wide-eyed child—where's the chrysalis you slept in?
When did the spark of spring melt down old winter snow?
Wise for spring not to tarry where my mind has been,
For summer craves the rainbow and the Monarch's glow.

My wide-eyed child—I know the wonders of your flight,
For I have seen the hills and meadows of my day.
Humbled is the breeze by the strength of your wings!
Dance by summer's light!
And I will keep our garden well, until my winter comes to stay.

A CANDLE ON FIRE

By Candlelight

I see the look of ecstasy
upon your face when we make love,
and wonder what you're thinking of
when you sigh, smile, and kiss my lips,
caress me with your fingertips.

I feel the fire of your love,
and your urgency for passion,
when we knead, mold, and fashion
legs and arms about each other,
while our dark light-figures hover.

I want to burn in your embrace,
hear your cries, feel you tremble,
as we tussle to resemble
the dance-moves of the breeze blown flame,
which casts our shadows without shame.

For that is how we want . . . and need . . . to love.

Candlelit Bedroom

When darkness falls upon your waiting bed,
And I, invited by your torrid eyes,
Am cast upon the walls by candle lights,
I'm changed;—I'm up! I'm returned from the dead!
I stretch away to where all shadows rise,
To dance this Tango born of heated nights.

Our limbs entwine, this night of burning nights,
Our half-lit figures springing from your bed!
We cast ourselves to where all angels rise,
As naked as the passion in your fiery eyes.
And changed are you, you've risen from the dead,
To flicker wildly like the twinkling lights!

We shape, misshape, reshape by dancing lights!
Your thighs, relieved of all their Summer's nights,
Entreat your breasts, pure envy of the dead,
To rise like mountains from your lusty bed!
Yes! I am slave to them, and to your eyes,
For they now show me how the shadows rise,

And how they blend, and fall, and once more rise.
Our bodies cry the tears of waxen lights,
Our moisture drops, like that of weeping eyes,
But we'll not weep this blesséd of all nights!
For darkness fell upon your longing bed,
And we have proved its springs are far from dead.

If locking groins keeps us from being dead—
Then locked we'll be, until our shadows rise
And helter-skelter dance above your bed!
Let's quake and quiver for the timid lights,
And dance the dances of forbidden nights,
And share the glory of the candle eyes.

A CANDLE ON FIRE

A dreamy gleam engulfs your sparkling eyes,
For we have merged and proved we're far from dead.
We've danced the music of Bolero nights!
And though we're spent, to love again we'll rise;
We'll shake once more the shadows of the lights,
Each time your passion fires your kindling bed!

Within your eyes my shadows fall and rise,
And 'til I'm dead, I'll dance by candle lights,
And hope my nights find heaven in your bed.

Cobalt Blue

Alumina! Oh, Alumina!
Pure and white!
What am I, a grayish
Cobalt fellow
Going to do?

If you give yourself,
To me, this night,
Together, you and I,
With great chemistry,
Will burn a Cobalt Blue!

Dilemma

Which deed is worse: My staying here with you,
Aware, in depth, this love is all your own,
To part, some day, for love I find is true?
Or, parting now, make done what you have known?
Equate the latter to a Dear's demise,
Where one is forced to grieve the corpse along,
And this will heal the essence of our lives.
This bears you life anew, to right a wrong,
For lingering can only raise the pain.
I cannot share what mine is not to give,
And falsely, to your heart, you will not gain
What most you crave, and this—you'll not forgive.
Prolonging love's demise is death delayed,
But quickly heals the wound that's swiftly made.

Eyes I Seek

Where hide the eyes whose vision has been made
For flight, if only once, to pierce my heart?
I've loved for sake of need, but always prayed
To need for sake of love, and there impart
A vision of my own. If eyes agree,
And such concordance sparks and fans the flame
Which carries flesh and soul to ecstasy,
Then gazed and gazer burn one heart the same.
These are the eyes I long to find, and will,
Some day, though seconds or a lifetime it
May take, for with one glance, my heart may still,
Yet beat forever though my life has quit.
Such eyes hold true the power of a spell,
To heaven find, or save a soul from hell.

Faith

I sit on the edge of a precipice wondering why
my love is far, far stronger than I,
and the rope is no thicker than a strand of hair,
yet I'm asked to take a leap out there.

Can I trust my heart and dare believe?
Is my vision true or do my eyes deceive?
I need to find out, and so—
here I go!

Flawless Love

Immortal Love is god to mortal man,
And perfect, whether men believe or not;
And treads without restraint, or master plan—
In mask—until unmasked by fallen heart.
But changed is not the face behind the guise!
Oh no! Disclosure merely lights the love
Who takes Love's place, and catches blinded eyes!
And thereafter, such changes shake and move
The lover and beloved, evermore,
Through temperate and tempestuous days.
And in the end, when Time taps on their door,
Time's moved by Love's true never dying ways.
The mask of Love no eyelets may possess,
Yet, flawless vision has it, nonetheless.

Free Fall

Your eyes, so beautiful a sky,
A cloudless heaven for my heart,
Endow my soul with wings to fly
Beyond the edges of the Earth.

Your eyes are rivals to the sun,
Make jealous every star at night;
And faster than the moon is spun
I hurtle towards their dazzling light.

I spiral down into your eyes—
To find the soul who sings to me!
To touch the flame it brings to me!

Oh, there I'll mingle breath with sighs;
And while you sleep I'll know I'm blessed,
For in your eyes my eyes have rest.

Hail, Woman

Hail, Woman, made of peonies and stone!
Your name gives birth to all that grows and dies.
No spring, without your loins, may spring alone,
Nor sunlight wrest the dazzle from your eyes!
To soothe the planter, and the planter's fruit,
Sweet Summer's bosom swells to Nature's call.
And by your very nature, life takes root,
Until uprooted by the chilling Fall.
You've clenched your teeth with pains of womanhood,
Now grasp the earth—because the earth is yours!
Drink deeply from yourself and taste the good,
For there you'll find the bounty of your shores.

Half a Love

If life had only favored us one love
Beyond all measure and compare, we would
Have found the joy two hearts can truly prove.
But one in love does not the other good.
Pursuing winter's breath can kill the spring,
And Spring is much too precious to ignore.
Pursue the fire of summer's offering,
Prepare for bounty autumn has in store,
And match your passion to a kindred flame.
Move past this heart, though caring it may be,
For it cannot ignite for you the same
Enthralling burn your essence begs of me.
A love must have two hearts in one allied,
But, I can't love, from lack of love, provide.

EDDIE MORALES

If You Were To Fall in Love with Me

If you were to fall in love with me,
Your heart would make your
Eyes ache for the sight of me,
Because seeing me would be
As necessary to your eyes
As breathing is to your body.

If you were to fall in love with me,
Your need to kiss me would overwhelm you,
And your desire for my kiss would be unbearable.
For the flavor of my lips, and tongue,
Would nourish your soul,
And would be like food and water
You require to survive.

If you were to fall in love with me,
You would not fear
The most intimate of my advances,
And I would plant kisses upon your eyes
When they are closed, and they would yearn for more;
And I would kiss every inch of your face,
And it would glow; I would bite your neck,
And you would grip me fiercely
With your passionate embrace.

But, I would not stop there.

My lips would find your breasts,
And you would offer them without shame.
And they would crave to be devoured.
My fingers would knead your body
And it would wave like the ocean.

Your form would be the terrain
My hands would explore.

A CANDLE ON FIRE

I would caress your back,
And move slowly down to your hips,
Where I would squeeze your flesh,
And pull you closer towards the urgency of our bodies.

And oh, what love-aroma you would have!
And oh, what sounds of love you would make!

I would sail along the smoothness of your thighs,
Which would burn with all the fires within you,
And I would touch those lips
Which prove you are all woman.
This passionate burning would provoke
The parting of your thighs,
Allowing me the ultimate of all intimacies.

And when you are ready,
You would pull me in,
And we would be as one,
And we would move as one,
And we would love as one,
And I would be the only heaven
You would need to know,

If you were to fall in love with me,
The way I have fallen in love with you.

In Your Absence

I can't exist outside of my dreams alone.

I can't tolerate inhaling the perfume
Of the wet land through the gray-filled haze,
Nor inhaling the smoke of a killing blaze,
While heading towards what will never come.

I can't accept being just another number—
Another digit no one will remember.
Life is a number . . . repeated a thousand times,
And then echoed a thousand times a thousand times.

I can't accept the eternal loneliness of a lighthouse
Or the stench of the foul-smelling gravel the undertow
Leaves behind at its feet, a sample of the Ocean's refuse,
Clinging to the ridges of my aging brow.

I can't accept the broken promises of some poor
Soul in love, who drags blame without words of distress,
And who vainly sheds tears that become more
Vainly shed with his newly found loneliness.

I can't accept an epitaph without sense.

I can't become the fly that marks the flies gone by.

I can't accept empty crockeries,
Cold crockeries of fading memories.

Yet, this is my world when you are gone.

I Roamed the Roads

I roamed the roads where red roses grew,
And freshly opened, one caught my eye.
I stopped to smell its petals, in dew,
And I soared above the sky.

Down to earth I landed, and clipped its stem.
It had no complaint about this intrusion;
But I was warned, by thorn, of a hearty problem,
Wherein grew confusion.

Its roots wrapped around my fallen heart,
The thorn, embedded within the same,
And ill I fell, ill, it fell apart,
Blackness, in my picking shame.

With time, I healed, by a homebound road,
Thorn, roots, and blackened petals gone.
Carefully, more wisely, there I strode,
Knowing well what could be done.

Along that path, a weed grew, eyeing me,
And seemed to plead, as it stood still,
In silence, for some kind of mercy,
By some power of my will.

I stayed well grounded, and up it flew,
Where after, there, I made my home.
And then, one day, into a tree it grew,
And from my heart, gone—my need to roam.

It Matters Not

Why should I fold and waste in hopelessness for beauty one lone woman may possess? Should I allow my face to wan and peak because her face is far from pale and bleak? Though she out-sun the beauty of a day, or far out-bloom all flowers grown in May, if not my eyes see beauty such as this, it matters not how beautiful she is.

Should I allow my heart to pine away because she's kind, and truly blinds the day? And has the nature of a gentle doe to go with lovely features all may know? Though all may see her humblest of her kind, and kinder than the kindest you may find, if she can never be that way with me, it matters not how friendly she can be.

Should I play dead? And let her virtues move my broken soul to perish for her love? Because her worthy life is greatly known, should I forget the value of my own? Though she is truly graced by God's own will, and fills more full-of-good than I can fill, if she can't see my goodness in all this, it matters not how truly good she is.

Because she thinks herself of noble birth, should I play fool and die for lack of worth? Such noble ranks think riches rank the best, and seek to court the best and shun the rest. The risk of falling's highest from above, but highest go the lowly when they love. Unless the proof is higher than the bar, it matters not how high and great they are.

In greatness, goodness, kindness, or the rest, I will not waiver in the final test; for if I find a love to suit my own, I'll die before her grieving tears are thrown. And If I find my courtship tossed away, I'll look, not back, but towards another day. For if our love was never meant to be, it matters *not* who keeps her love from me.

Juxtaposition

love:

a light
a sound
an aroma
a spoken word
a feeling

losing:

your heart,
your mind
your body
your soul

hate is:

all of the above

minus

love

Love and Honey

Love is like honey sweetly dripping.
No bee engenders tastier dew.
Lovers: delight in digit dipping
And savor this nectar through and through.

No bee oozes delectable dew
Like the daisy bathed in passion's mist.
To savor this nectar, through and through,
Drink of the mead sweet life has kissed.

Like the daisy bathed in passion's mist,
Love emits feverish condensation.
Imbibe the mead sweet life has kissed
And favor the dew its consummation.

Love radiates keen condensation;
Lovers: revel in digit dipping!
Until the dew finds consummation,
Love is like honey, sweetly dripping.

Mugunghwa

So many roses has Borinquen,
my Estrella of Busan,
but none have taken sight away,
or captured well the heart of man,
like on the day I gazed upon
a goddess from a foreign sea,
and lost, to you, both heart and sight,
beneath a whispering mango tree.

(I'll listen to the mango trees)

I pray each day our love endures,
but suns have ways of slipping by,
and every night, of fleeting nights,
brings closer our one last goodbye.

But how do melded hearts depart?

How may you leave and linger here?

How do we cross these boundaries
our kinfolk hold so close and dear?

(And hold them close and ever dear)

Traditions bid we keep the sacred
order of our ways intact,
yet hearts like ours, which moved
beyond the sea, for sake of love, must act.

So, I will sing for you a song,
and we will step this waltz for two,
And we will love until the end,
until the stars weep over you.

EDDIE MORALES

(And I, too, will weep for you)

When last we meet, this final night,
I'll bring to you a rose bouquet,
in water from a silver stream,
collected at the end of day;
and all *coquis* will pitch their tune,
to speak of one with almond eyes,
and voice no angel can resist,
of one who brightened up the skies

(You, who brightened up my skies)

With joyful laughter, carefree smiles,
and heart so true and ever pure;
of one who carries her own pain, and
for the sake of home, endures
what must be done for honor's sake,
but who has seen the mango tree
and tasted of its wondrous fruit,
and takes now home a part of me.

(And when you're home, remember me)

Despite how Fate has seen it fit,
for now let's melt in tight embrace,
And kiss, a kiss—a lasting kiss;
then let me gaze upon your face,
So I may paint my mind with you,—
your eyes, and lips, and silken hair—
until your image, etched upon my soul,
forever keeps you there.

(For love, forever, keeps me there)

My Garden of Roses

The early morning sun
provokes the eyes,
while warbling robins raise
a waking tune,
to stir the soul
to greet one's dearest lives,
in yawn, and stretch,
like roses striking bloom.

Sweetly they do wake
these essences of mine.
they rise above bold mountains—
rocky, steep, and tall,
leap across wide oceans—
adding nectar to the brine.
spread petals over windy vales,
like oak trees in the fall.

And each and every morning,
my garden stirs anew,
and nightly my frail roses
are safely tucked away.

May their auras never fail
to glow the whole night through,
So I can dream,
and pray to see,
another light of day.

My Little Smile

That teddy is not made for girls of twelve,
But you have hopes, as pre-teens often do,
In front of a reflection made to delve
For all the secrets deep inside of you.

When will your womanly attributes arrive?
They've yet to come!
Take your time!

That you'll become a woman is too true.
There will be changes, but I'll see no change.
Those womanly formations will not hide you,
No matter how you shape and rearrange.

I'm just afraid your eyes will change as well.
It's a girl's inevitability,
To trade Dad's image for another's spell,
And I must have the heart to let you see.

You've yet to grow.
Don't hurry.
Take your time.

Next Chapter

My bookmark rests on chapter
twenty-three.

It's on this chapter
my love abandoned me.

The chapter after that
is blank.

Ergo,

I don't know yet
whom I should thank.

Nightingale

A Nightingale lands on a branch outside
my open window one sunny morning.

I offer water,
food, an open hand,
but she doesn't budge,
and she remains silent.

I speak kindly, softly, and not a note.

I ask: What ails you? Have I offended you?

When I move away from the window she turns her head
as if to keep an eye on me. She waits.

Feeling rejected, I begin to sing a melancholy song.

The Nightingale then flutters to my windowsill,
settles down, closes her eyes…
and listens.

A CANDLE ON FIRE

Our Silhouettes

A shadow lives where light cannot alight,
And revels in the darkness of its shade,
And sings to all the spirits of the night
A dusky tune, a silent serenade.
But shadows need our forms to give them spring,
To give them shape and shapelessness the same,
To give them hope of wanton frolicking,
So they may dance the tango of a flame.
Let passion strike our forms against the wall!
Or ceiling! Or the mirrors of our eyes!
And from our bed, the dance floor of the ball,
Let's give the shadows motion for their lives.
Let us embrace before the candle's eye,
And cast our silhouettes upon the sky.

Silent Agony

Your secret is as deep as ocean wide,
Yet evident as if upon your sleeve.
Your eyes betray what in your heart you hide,
But speaking of this truth is but to grieve.
Unspoken words restrain their need for air,
For if they're voiced, no echo will they hear.
And this is far too great for ears to bear,
And far too cruel to bear from one so dear.
There's no reward of pain for things unsaid,
So silence moves the center of your heart.
Beyond all hope, you'll find you're nearly dead,
For silence also tears the soul apart.
If spoken, nothing gained, unspoken, too,
Then better to be mute to love untrue.

Snow on Christmas Eve

For days, the children prayed for snow to come.
They dreamed of stars, all Frisbee-sized, to make
The biggest balls of white they'd ever seen.
They didn't care if fingers might go numb,
Or whether tongues should catch a falling flake,
Or winter's breath came whooshing through this scene.

They craved a time for fun, for running through
A field of heaven's dust, for skis and sleds,
As well as time for snowballs and the fight!
They longed to play, and yell, build snowmen too,
While Christmas angels made their earthly beds,
And cherubs dreamt of earth, all milky white.

Their wish came true, and snow fell Christmas Eve —
A heavy feather dusting of the world.
Within an hour, a world immaculate
Was hung before my eyes, and I could breathe
Again the radiant air, which God had purled.
I knew, this must be what it's like at Heaven's gate.

Sometimes Love

Sometimes love strikes like a cat,
Pouncing on its prey.
It leaps, lands, claws your soul,
Then shreds your heart away.

Once its belly is sated,
Love calmly departs,
To seek another fool
To add to broken hearts.

The Flame

The moth and I have equal plight:
We take to flight—
To seek the flame
That sears the frame
With ever heightening delight.

The moth continues its endeavor.
Far from clever!
The landing's quick,
And in a tick,
Poor moth is doomed and gone forever.

To burn in ecstasy is swell,
But know the spell:
To quench desire,
Fight fire with fire,
So that the flame's consumed as well.

Transfiguration

Are you okay, Sweetie? Are you okay?
Think you can make it through another day?

  I really don't know, Mama, but I can try,
  'Cause it's hard to live when I have to die.

Are you okay, Sugar? Do you want to talk?
We can sit right here, or we can take a walk.

  Here's okay, Mama, case I have to cry,
  'Cause it's hard to walk when I have to die.

Are you okay, Darlin'? May I comb your hair?
Do you want it simple, or with a little flair?

  Either's fine, Mama, use a nice black tie,
  'Cause I can't be ugly when I have to die.

Are you okay, Sweetheart? Do you want some food?
I made you Peach Cobbler and it's awfully good.

  No thank you, Mama, don't want no pie,
  'Cause it's hard to eat when I have to die.

Honey, are you okay? Are you okay, Honey?
I can tell you a story and make it funny.

  Don't matter, Mama, I'll moan and sigh,
  'Cause it's hard to laugh when I have to die.

Are you okay, Baby? Don't you fall asleep.
'Cause if you do I'll surely weep.

  I have to . . . Mama . . . it's time to die . . .
  'Cause my wings are ready and I have to fly!

Unanswered Questions

Exhilarating were the moments
of confident desire,
the fiery, inebriating words
of the most glorious of all emotions,
and my heart found solace
behind their blinding mist.

Then the blinding mist,
like a cataract,
grew thicker,
and it took from me a little,
then a little more,
and then finally all.

The words, once a crashing tide,
a raging river, lava spewing out of
an impassioned volcano,
drowned in some abyss
beneath an unknown sea.

Sometimes, there are colder things beating
within the core of human flesh
than are swimming in
the deepest trenches
of the darkest of oceans.

Wasted Nights

The stars hang twinkling in the sky,
Presenting each a sparkling eye,
But when my eyes your eyes espy,
Each jealous star begins to cry,
Until we waste the night.
Oh, green becomes the silver Moon,
With moonbeams helter-skelter strewn
Like fireflies in nights of June,
Until we waste the night.

Come let your arms share my embrace;
Let lips on lips be ours to grace:
Take kisses where our fingers trace
Our bodies laid on silk and lace.
Until we waste the night—
Let's give the candle needed fire!
To blend our shadows with desire,
And climb our passion ever higher
Until we waste the night.

Allow my breath your breath to take,
Let all beneath us creak and quake,
Let all foundations therein break,
With every gesture we may make,
Until we waste the night.
And once we've made of night the most,
And in our dreams our eyes are lost,
We'll hear our pillows sigh and boast:
"How they've wasted here tonight!"

What I Have Learned

Pain and sorrow can
be replaced by things unsought

There is a storm
within the warmest of eyes

There is a life giving force
behind the gentlest of lips

And if one dares anew,
one can sink into that storm,
breathe, and live again

Wild Orchid

Beloved's ample beauties overflowed,
And stretched vivid the imagination;
And swelled natural my predilection
To nuzzle in a flower so peak endowed.

Her ravenous, moist, and biting lips threw
My soul into a river I adore,
And rabidly laid promise to outpour
The essence every orchid strives to brew.

Such sweet aching charged her musky lair!
I left her moaning lips for muted lips—
Where tongue and lips indulged in fleshy sips—
While maiden petals breathed the lusty air!

Oh! Well knew east and west Beloved's knees,
While headed north to south, my love and I!
Where forcefully we lingered, sigh for sigh,
'til frantic hips released our tortured tease.

The nectar flowed between her supple hills,
And brought her momentary peace of mind;
She quivered like a leaf inside the wind,
So tempered by the storm and heaven spills.

I—reveled in our tantalizing deaths!
But reveling brought reveling anew!
And newly my beloved sought to brew
Her nectar, stilled from passion's burning depths.

Beloved turned a Kama Sutran page—
And then another, and another still!
Until I lost control, along with will,
And noisily embraced her mounted rage!

A CANDLE ON FIRE

And in the end, what more can two lives give?
But every drop of life to full extent—
The Orchid dies when Nature's dew is spent,
And spending is to conquer death—and live!

When Love Rests

Should Love, for any reason, dare to rest,
It cannot save itself from Death's cold hand.
No half-lit flame exists which burns the best.
No half-kiss sears the lips it seeks to land!
To ever burn must be the life of Love;
Forever true it must keep Nature's fire;
And never fail to light the heart, or glove
The heated passions of this great desire.
Or else, Death finds a way to kill the flame;
Or tepid turns the soul which fiercely burned;
Or barely will it live a cripple, lame.
For when Love rests, it means the road has turned.
As kin to perseverance, keep the course,
Or Love, from whom it loved, will bear divorce.

Yours is the Face

Your face, my love, the countenance I've yearned too long to see,
Is perfect for my eyes; it soothes my sight like drink for thirst.
Now, other visages within my gaze are false to me,
And real's the dream, that in my nights, my soul has nursed.
And here you are, a foreign land, which came to me instead,
So I could travel little in my quest to find a place —
Where eyes can melt all winter ice and bosom rest my head;
Where kisses cool and sear the same with heaven's blessed grace.
You are the right to any wrong, which so far crossed my heart,
And level path to rocky roads that steer a man astray.
You are the source of every seedling's hope to make a start;
You're honesty, and goodness, which will soothe me through each day.
No longer need my eyes, though time detracts, a better sight
Than this, your face, which gives me sun by day and moon by night.

TETRADS OF SONNETS

A CANDLE ON FIRE

Tetrad I: Passion, Sonnet I

BEGINNINGS

The spark that lights the heart inflames the eye
With sparkle stars must envy and adore.
This sight of love-at-first brings passion nigh,
And scorches every lover to their core.
Thereafter, lover and beloved dance
As one—in touch, in sight, in lips consumed.
The Moon is ever brighter for romance,
The Sun resplendent, flowers more perfumed.
Such splendid agony when all is new!
The agony! when fingers long to touch!
And lovers must imbibe their lover's brew,
For in that nectar, Life has poured so much.
Beginnings know that passion must begin
When sparkling eyes reveal the fire within.

Tetrad I: Passion, Sonnet II

Prelude to an End

How quickly fades a lover's dazzling light!
A lantern, lit by passion, must be fed
Continuously! Kept forever bright!
Or with the night, the light of day is dead.
Communication is the key to love:
With words a body writes without a word;
With smiles that make a lover pause and move;
With torrid eyes that hunger to be heard;
While listening is lock to hold the key!
But somehow, lover and beloved fail
To burn as one; and neither hear nor see
The agony their ailing lights entail.
The flicker of a flame begins to fade
When passion begs for life, but death is paid.

Tetrad I: Passion, Sonnet III

Ending

Such sadness veils those fallen out of heart
When sparkling eyes, so dimmed by passion's death,
Reclaim first sight, and lovers tear apart
With every deed that once gave love its breath.
A soothing touch turns crawling under skin.
The image in one's eye turns sight opaque.
A kiss transforms to ash the flame within
And heading back finds sealed all paths you take.
Are lost the days of sunshine and the moon?
It seems they go the way of day and night,
For roads too wide must fork, and all too soon,
Thereafter, comes the dimming of the light.
An ending brings a chill to flood one's core
When passion dies and burns love's flame no more.

Tetrad I: Passion, Sonnet IV

New Beginning

The Phoenix and the Flame are kindred souls,
And strangers not to Passion's burning depths.
The Sun, though dead by night, again consoles
The world at morning time, with newborn breaths.
So why not find Beloved flame anew?
Or Lover, find another source of light?
Perchance, relight the embers Passion knew,
And keep familiar lanterns burning bright?
Un-fork the road behind or move along!
But waste no time! For Time is quick to fly!
Rely upon the ember's crackling song!
And burn a sparkle in a lover's eye!
To burn away is Passion's sole desire,
When lovers, like the Phoenix, love the fire.

Tetrad II: Hands, Sonnet I

Baby Hands

A newborn needs no reason to exist
Except the reason Life's compelled to give.
Its hand, so frail, disposed to make a fist,
Appears to say, "I have a right to live!"
And both will cling to mother's soothing breast
By instinct than by knowledge of the act.
With time, these hands advance, are put to test.
In grasping, they inspect what hands attract.
They catch a fall; they grip another's hand,
Or set to rest if nothing goes their way.
They must be held if danger's in command
And made to stretch at length when safe to play.
Such fragile hands will learn of fists and prayer,
When knowing hands are called to take them there.

Tetrad II: Hands, Sonnet II

Hands of Youth

Adventure is the life of youthful hands—
Exploring all that needs to be explored!
They roil the waters, make their own demands,
And every step's a challenge to be scored.
If failure slaps the hands that stray too far,
The peaceful breast may soothe them once again;
But settled hands know where to set the bar—
So youthful ones find comfort from their pain—
So newly armed, and venturing anew,
They vanquish all that troubled them before.
The clock is always ticking Time's ado,
And hands, still soft, have yet to do much more.
O hands of youth! How fast you slip away!
When Time's own pulse beats down the light of day.

Tetrad II: Hands, Sonnet III

Mature Hands

Ah, settled hands, caress a youthful face.
Embrace, with ring upon your finger—Love.
Bethink, in times of woe, a joyful place
Of moments held in prayer, of Saints to move.
Release from mind and heart the angered fist;
Discard the weapon War needs to survive.
Be gentle, when your essences insist
On holding own; act quickly to forgive.
Collect all petals fallen on the mind;
Reveal them when familial moments rise.
And keep, at hand, all friendships you may find,
For they hold cures for pain and tearful eyes.
The well aged hands, and hands of youth, are blest
When those between them both, by love, are pressed.

Tetrad II: Hands, Sonnet IV

Well Aged Hands

These hands have served their younger master well,
But Life soon leads them over golden pond,
Where, like the baby's hands, their frailties tell;
Where youth, now wrinkled, shriveled, and beyond
Repair, is petal precious on the mind.
But nobler hands await them in the end—
All knowing Hands, that well-aged hands will find,
Who care not whether theirs are slow to bend,
Or ever walk another mortal strand.
For first, a soul's let go to find its birth,
And in return, must grasp the Lord's fair hand
Anew, and loosen memories of Earth.
Eternal are the gifts of love and grace,
When hands, unbound, touch God's immortal face.

Tetrad III: My Obsession with Poetry, Sonnet I

To K.C. from Shakespeare

That he's "obsessed" is far too mildly put.
His personalities are split in three,
Within his mind; and I, The Bard, am out
To see him justice done—his part of me.
Young Romeo gave life for Juliet,
And Juliet's own death achieved both ends;
But oh, that "flaw" was theirs the day they met!
One loses loves, and may, as well, lose friends,
But Poetry you will not lose! Why not
This art enkindle such a flame to scorch
The mind the way a love can sear the heart?
Too many, now, have watered passion's torch,
So, though obsession may be "tragic" curse,
Know, we are tragically in love with verse.

Tetrad III: My Obsession with Poetry, Sonnet II

To L.J.S. from Poe in Regards to My Dark Side

I, too, must here confess a morbid thought,
For sake of our obsession with the dark.
We are a coin, and with it have been bought
The faces which the good and bad will spark.
A loftiness we find without the light,
We've seen the Raven blackness of the night,
But dreams, like my Lenore, can keep us whole.
Sit down, and mark your sufferings and pain,
Without restraint, though ebon flows the ink
From out your heart, like clouds let loose the rain,
To pour away what poison you may drink.
Go, pen the words, speak them line by line,
For even darkness may bring words divine.

Tetrad III: My Obsession with Poetry, Sonnet III

To A.C.S. from Millay in Regards to my Feminine Side

I am his softer side, but oh, my friend—
We burn the candle always day and night!
His star and mine are but one single blend
Of passion for this Art of highest light!
The joy! What joy! (Like mother's babe in womb),
I may, with verse, have given birth to him,
But if you cut the cord, he takes the tomb,
For without verse, love-like, his life is grim.
Our souls have both the fire no one can quell,
And though the Scythe-Man has me now, some say
Our spirits will engage to verse a spell,
As fellow poets, eon and a day.
If, with his torch, he passes on this flame,
Eternity may hail, and speak, his name.

Tetrad III: My Obsession with Poetry, Sonnet IV

To Shakespeare, Poe, and Millay

No greatness has been ever reached without
Obsession for an art which burns the mind!
This passion's my obsession, which, no doubt,
Has all our spirits ever intertwined—
In favor of this noblest form for words.
Now hear, these words are mine, and mine alone,
For yours have long been wreathed by fame's accord,
Within your time, and mine are not yet done.
I praise your passion, burning in me too!
I praise your words, which always serve me well!
I praise you for the path you've charmed me through!
But now, I take the torch, to cast my spell,
And write my verses, all that I can give,
Forever hopeful, when I die, I live!

SLAMMIN' AWAY

A CANDLE ON FIRE

Poetry Slams

I like going to poetry slams because I can say anything I want, about whatever I want, and no one gives a damn; because people who go to poetry slams don't give a damn what you say, so long as you have something to say.

I can slam anything, and everything, from the mundane to the miraculous, from A to Z, from birth to death, from here to there, to nowhere and everywhere, from atheism to religion to politics, and no one gives a damn, because poetry slammers don't give a damn what you say, so long as you have something to say.

I can sit in on a poetry slam and listen to the black man rant about racial injustice, the Korean woman laud her exoticness, the Irish lass Riverdance to life, the English bloke talk about the Royal Family, the Aussie go crocodile hunting in the outback, the Japanese live the haiku, the Puerto Rican man speak of his lady, his jibarita, the Hindu woman sing a golden poem, and even a man from Iraq profess he is an American, and no one gives a damn, because poetry slammers don't give a damn what you say, so long as you have something to say.

I can sit in on a poetry slam and listen to the voice of the Jew, the Catholic, the Baptist, the Pentecostal, the Protestant, the Hindi, the Buddhist, the Lutheran, the evangelist, the born again Christian, and the Muslim, and all the rest of the religious denominations, and no one gives a damn, because poetry slammers don't give a damn what you say, so long as you have something to say.

I can sit in on a poetry slam and see the rape, the murder, the car-jacking, the stabbing, the child abuse, the drug addiction, the hatred, and no one gives a damn, because poetry slammers don't give a damn what you say, so long as you have something to say.

I can sit in on a poetry slam and see the love, the friendship, the sensual, the sexual, the birth of a child, the touch of a loved one, I can see a mother, a father, a wife, a husband, a brother, a sister, an uncle, an aunt, a

A CANDLE ON FIRE

grandfather, a grandmother, and all that is family, all that is of the human condition, and no one gives a damn, because no one at a poetry slam gives a damn what you say, so long as you have something to say.

And then, in going from one poetry slam to another, an idea began to ferment inside my mind, and then it hit me. I came to a realization — not just an epiphany, but a paradox within an epiphany. I realized you and I, me and you, we, are not at all alike. I realized you and I, me and you, we, are a lot alike. And in a poetry slam, we may not give a damn what anyone says, as long as they have something to say, but I also realized we come to poetry slams because—WE GIVE A DAMN!

EDDIE MORALES

Bang!

I may be a poor boy from the south of Da Bronx,
But don't be classifyin' me as one of Da Punks.
I'm not out there gangin' nor am I bangin' the block,
And I'm not one to go around carryin' a Glock.
No, no, no, no, no, no, no!

I want somethin' better from a poet's education
So I can be a model for my next generation.
You wanna battle with me,
without committin' a crime?
Come on—poet-to-poet—let us do it in rhyme!

Think yer verses are cruisin'?
Well yer in for a bruisin'

Think yer rhymes are all tight?
Well yer in for a fight

Think yer ready and able?
Well I'm Cain and yer Abel.

Now, think yer skillin' and willin'?
Well I've got news for you buddy,
I'll be doin' the killin'!

'Cause I'm a mean mutha versin' rhymin' son-of-a-`gun,
Who's got a three-fifty-seven of a fiery tongue!
My rhymes'll have ya bleedin' by the time that I'm done,
'Cause I'm a mean mutha versin' rhymin' son-of-a-gun!

Didn't hear it then? Well I'm a say it again!

A CANDLE ON FIRE

I'm a mean mutha versin' rhymin' son-of-a-gun,
I eat rhymers for breakfast just to have me some fun,
And not even light can travel at the speed of my tongue,
'Cause I'm a mean mutha versin' rhymin' son-of-a-gun!

But don't get discouraged, I don't want you to quit.
All I really wanna do is teach ya to spit.
But better run for cover, better sound the alarm,
'Cause when it comes to rhymin'---I'm a nuclear bomb!

'Cause I'm a mean mutha versin' rhymin' son-of-a-gun,
I can spit out ten to just yer one,
Before ya know it, I'll have ya on the run,
'Cause I'm a mean mutha versin' rhymin' son-of-a-gun!

And I listen, listen, listen,

I listen to the rappers and their songs from the crapper.
Well they can rhyme to the gutter while I make mine all dapper.
Without me dissin' my women, or me swimmin' in curses,
I'll be primpin' my rhymin' with my eloquent verses.

I've got Masters behind me, like my Frosty and Shakes,
Who come to lend me their Muses 'cause they know what it takes.
I've got Browning, Auden, St. Vincent Millay,
Who also come a-callin' just to show me the way.

I've got Bishop and Plath—
So get out of my path!

I've got Dante and Keating—
Just to give you a beatin'!

I've got Dunbar and Poe—
So your rhyme's gonna go!

How about now, think yer skillin' and willin'?
I've got news for ya buddy—

EDDIE MORALES

I'll still, still, be doin' the killin'!

'Cause I'm a mean mutha versin' rhymin' son-of-a-gun,
Who's got a three-fifty-seven of a fiery tongue!
My rhymes'll have you bleeding by the time that I'm done,

'Cause I'm a mean

BANG!

Mutha versin'

BANG! BANG!

Rhymin'

RAT-TAT-TAT-TAT-TAT!

SON-OF-A-GUN!

Now, get outta my face, you're all dead.

BANG!

Cool Cat

He poured himself onto the stage like freshly brewed coffee,
all the rage, black shades to match the color of his skin,
pearly whites contrasting the out and in,
and while the Jazz flowed, the din died,
so all the poets in the house could hear and see.
You can't be judged by what you're thinking,
but once you open your mouth, you will be judged.
Lauded? Maybe. Or verbally jostled, poked, and nudged,
maybe even harangued by snapping fingers,
so he chose his words carefully, because—
they represented all that he was.

He spilled his poem with such satiny eloquence,
each and every word tightly knitted,
each in turn a relevant sequence pitted
one against the other, and from the baby grand
sitting in the front, hypnotized,
to the knockout way in the back, mesmerized,
everyone had the sugar in their coffee stirred, and I thought,
"I see you! I hear you! And I feel you, my Brother!"

He rattled the chains of his ancestors with great finesse,
Exposing the ragged flesh wounds of their souls,
because they would not acquiesce
to the iniquities perpetrated by their tormentors,
and I thought, "I see that!"
He laid on me the words to their freedom,
and I thought, "I hear that!"
But the chains rattled alongside them for decades still,
against their will, and I thought,
"I know where you're coming from with that."

EDDIE MORALES

Then, next to me, a pink lady, her dome topped with wispy cotton,
whispered loud enough for me to hear,
"I don't understand this "black thing!"
Well, I knew the turmoil a comment like that could bring,
but for that moment I thought it best forgotten
than to roil the waters, because not
everything you hear is peaches and cream,
and not everything you see is what it seems.
And I whispered back,
"Sometimes, in order to understand this thing
or that, you have to 'be' this thing
or that! Or, vicariously live this thing
or that. And maybe in order for you
to understand this 'black thing,' you
have to 'be' black."

Meanwhile, the poet, after spilling the last drop,
was applauded, and afforded praises like "off the hook,"
"unreal," and "that was phat," after which, he proceeded
to announce me, and called me up, and I poured myself
onto that stage like cold milk into a tall glass,
and I remember thinking, as I approached the Mic,
"That Dude is one cool cat."

Well, we slapped hands, pounded fists, and
leaned into each other, and after having finished our
"mano a mano," I pointed two fingers his way,
and wished him, "Peace, my Brother."
And he placed one hand over his heart,
and respectfully replied,
"Con mucho amor, mi amigo Borincano."

Perfect Universe

Well knows the Cosmos the origin
of the Cartesian coordinate system,
and the Universe gives us a sign, (s-i-n-e)
and many others, to that effect;
and the Galactic Systems formulate,
and establish, the borders
of our solar system within infinity.

The Earth is coordinately challenged, leaving Nature
Unable to use the universal calculator, and it goes off on a
tangent, and Nature uses memory and pencil,
allowing a rogue gene to collide with paradise.

Nature figures out man, by decimal point placement,
or misplacement, and man figures into the equation,
(this seen-and-unseen-fearing man);
and by triangulation finds his Eden cubed.

Paradise expands to the horizon,
and each step leads to a question,
and each answer leads to an exponentiation
of questions seeking answers.

But in the search for more answers,
man corrupts the equation
with the inception of the mathematical mind,
and the perimeter of paradise perishes.

Did the creator create the created?
Or the created create the creator?
Were both created by the infinite
probabilities of the universe?

Where begins or ends the diameter
of the universe anyway?

EDDIE MORALES

Why is the diameter of man's
world infinitely shorter?
And where sleeps the unseen deity?

The seen leads the way to the unseen and back.
Minded seeds planting minded seeds, bearing minded fruit!

The cogent division of the land intersected
is dissected by the mindless minded burrowing minds,
and the exponentially burrowing minds,
bearing exponentially burrowing minds
bearing . . .

The mushroom fires blame nuclear combustion.
The colliding tectonic plates blame nuclear contusion.
The gelatinizing children blame nuclear intrusion.

Blame it on the Cosmos!
Blame it on the Universe!
Blame it on the Galaxy!
Blame it on the Solar System!
Blame it on the Earth!
Blame it on the nature of things,
but don't blame man?
The corrupter of the equation?

If paradise was the beginning,
And Man was kicked out of paradise,
then perdition is the logical conclusion!

Man must become extinct.

And then, the final equation makes
the Cosmos perfectly balanced:
Death equals the return to paradise—
free of deity
and free of man!

Litany of Clichés

I will not abandon ship,
For after the rains, there are rainbows,
Especially here, in America,
The melting pot of the world,

Where someone's always the apple
Of someone's eye, and it's a living hell,
A shot in the dark.

But, better late than never, for I am
A black sheep, speaking what comes to my mind,
And writing it down exactly the same way I
Thought about it, and nothing needs to be changed,
It is perfect. It's like the blind leading the blind,

The same with the broken heart, but there's the calm
Before the storm, and like the caterpillar that turns
Into a butterfly, I'm always chasing rainbows.

I always look for clouds with silver linings
Even if they are cold as ice, or maybe cold-hearted.
No! Maybe warm-blooded! It's crystal clear to me now.

This is because I dance to the beat of a different drummer!
Or is it the same drummer with a different beat?

What the hell! It's always darkest before dawn,
Because Death is the gateway to life, and
Every rose has it thorns.

I can look into the eye of the needle, but
If the camel can't fit, will I? For I am,
After all, fat as a pig and this makes me afraid,
For fear makes you run, no, stay, no, yes, run,
And I must follow my heart, and make

EDDIE MORALES

Footprints in the sand,
From the bottom of my heart.

I will go against the current!
For it is God's mysterious way!
It is God's will! Jesus be praised!

Good things come to those who wait,
For good things come in tiny packages,
So don't be in a hurry, for haste makes waste!

Oh, boy, do I have a heart of stone, and it's hell,
And hell comes from inside, no, from outside,
No, from downside, no wait, from upside…my head,

And Hell hath no freakin' fury like some woman scorned!
And there's hell to pay for it, when I'm on a high horse,
Where I can be myself, you can be yourself,
She can be herself, he can be herself,
(Yes, nowadays he can be herself)
And dogs and cats can be themselves.

Hallelujah!
Amen, Brother!
Amen, Sister!
Amen!

Now, I can't change the past,
Because I did it my way, not your way,
Not his way, not her way,
Not the professor's way!
No way!

I know, if at first you don't succeed,
If it doesn't kill you,
I'll always love you, I'll always remember.
After all, I'm only human,
And I will never forget you!

A CANDLE ON FIRE

And I know, deep in my heart,
Kissing is a game. Honestly,
This is my original conclusion.

But I will find the light at the end of the tunnel,
Unless I'm dead, then I won't go into the light,
No, I won't! Don't you go into the light
Either, Carol Ann! The Poltergeist will get you!

Ah, but Carol Ann's mom and I fit like
Hand and glove, like shoe and foot,
Like galoshes and rain, like snow
And snow plow, grass and lawnmowers.
And her lips are red like roses.

And boy, do I love life.
Life is like…
Life goes…
Life has…
Life does…
Life lends…
Life finds…
Life this…
Life that…
Ah, yes, tell me one more time,
Why don't you?

I knew a little angel once.
I knew a little devil, once.
But, lo and behold! I'm a lone wolf!

But, shhh, I have a secret.
I found out love is like a rose,
And the man in the mirror is me!
And I'm here, somewhere in
Freakin' Never-never land!
But nobody's perfect.

If I don't have any guts,

EDDIE MORALES

I'll have no glory!
And if I'm not in pain, I'm
Not going to gain I don't know what.
Whoopee freakin' do!

I fear nothing, except of course, FEAR!
Be afraid, yourself, be very afraid!
But let's take it one day at a time.
No, let's take it one step at a time, instead.
No, no, let's take BABY steps.
Let's crawl before we walk.
Let's walk before we run.
Let's cross at the green and not in between!
Why don't we?

However, there are other fish in the sea.
So let's pull the plug on the ocean and
Gather up those fishies.

I know, I know, parting is such sweet sorrow.
I'm really going to miss you, NOT!
Because you're going to miss ME!

I'm so sorry for what I just did,
I put all of my eggs into one basket.
It fell, and now I have an omelet.
Oh, a tisket and a tasket, I
Dropped my freakin' yellow basket!

Sorry again, it's just that my love
Is pure as a dove, but she's not even
A freakin' virgin anymore!
I made sure of that!

Okay, okay! I'll be quiet as a mouse.
I guess I'm running on empty.
And shit happens, sooner or later!
Why? Because I'm looking, once again,
For my freakin' soul mate!

A CANDLE ON FIRE

You know, I tried looking for those streets of gold,
And can't find one! Where are they?
There's no word. There must be a reason.

Oh, Shakespeare, I know the world's a stage,
But could you take this thorn from out my side,
And get me off this freakin' stage!
I feel like I'm dying up here.

But, through thick and thin,
I like to tilt at windmills,
And tomorrow is another day,
And I've put in my two cents,
And I feel as ugly as that stupid duckling,
And until hell freezes over,
Or pigs fly,
I know waiting is the hardest part,
And I know God is watching from above,
(This rhymes with love)
(The way snow rhymes with go)
And we are each alone.
Although, some fit together like flies on sh…
(Okay, forget that one)
And when it rains, it pours.
(Not the way clumpy salt pours)
For when the going gets tough,

I work like a dog, and you'll have a place
In my heart, because you know you
Make my heart sing, you're
My one and only,
You're the light of my life,
The wind beneath my wings,
The chewing gum beneath my shoes,
(Alright, alright, forget that one too!)

Because, when all is said and done,
I get this feeling of déjà vu.

Misdirection

So tiny, barely using up the crib,
A mother lifts and takes her son to breast,
Then stops his pangs, with nipple in his mouth,
And there, contentedly, his urges rest.

So cute, she thinks, his desperate suckling sounds,
As if he'll never, ever drink once more;
He stops, and breathes a dozen breaths in one,
While mother hugs the angel she adores.

He opens up his eyes, two stars so bright,
And she is awed by everything he is—
His ten whole fingers, all ten toes as well,
The smell of powder when she gives a kiss.

She slips a hand beneath his neck so frail,
Afraid too strong a grip will make it snap,
While in her other hand his bottom sits,
And with great care, she puts him on her lap.

She dreams of all the things he's going to do,
So quaint, like turning over on the bed,
Then crawling, walking, saying his first words;
With "Momma," hopefully, the first one said.

Of course will come more "firsts" all know so well:
First year, first step, first potty-training day;
The first day of Pre-K, a scary time
For some, afraid to see you go away.

If only Time would creep along somehow,
And we could double every second on
The clock, and this way, keep them twice as long,
Before they grow, and cuteness is all gone.

A CANDLE ON FIRE

But, babies don't stay babies very long.
And by an observation, quite astute,
You must enjoy their cuteness, while you can,
For even Mother Dahmer thought her Jeffrey cute!

The Challenge

Come, tell me your story, master of prose.
Use elements of the proper language
To sway me to your side, and if all goes
Well, hallowed will your words be on the page.

So many things in common do we share,
Like our emotional sincerity,
Our love for beauty, and our honest care
For words, which have such unbound purity.

But I feel we can take our prose higher.
It is the basis of my argument,
For my rhymes, and it's my greatest desire
That all may hear what I so here present.

It is my intention to speak clearly,
Not to chide, or ever to belittle
All that you endeavor, but if dearly
You love this art form, it takes a little

Practice, perseverance, patience, and time,
To get it right. No one's born omniscient,
And this relates to poetry, to fine
Prose, so words in practice are words well spent.

Surely, the point must be perfectly clear.
The best poetry I have ever heard
Have echoed words like music to my ears,
Have rhymes that now I cherish word for word.

A CANDLE ON FIRE

There's no doubt a poem is a poem
When the echoed words, good or bad, are there.
With prose, I don't know what to make of them,
Most being simply stories—dry, threadbare.

Our rhymes are much like couples seeking love,
Or loved ones making complements of two,
Who, together, synergistically move
To do what not one single word can do.

They are much like couples on the dance floor,
Each part of every pair well synchronized
With the other, each one being much more
As part of two than one soul can realize.

We may begin our verses without rhyme,
To get our bearings, and to figure out
What we want to say, but let's take the time
To move one step higher, and leave no doubt

That what we've written is more than a prose,
Blank verse, or free verse poem; let's echo,
And we'll be remembered longer than those
Poets who don't, and care less to do so.

But, it's okay if gift for rhyme is lacking,
And your Muses bar this undertaking,
For I've seen it happen, time after time,
              That they will surely prose who cannot rhyme.

The Hanging Limerick

And Other Such Nonsense

A CANDLE ON FIRE

The Hanging Limerick One

I have a dilemma perturbing.
You might even call it disturbing.
Oh, my limericks are rich,
But that fifth line's a bitch!
—

The Hanging Limerick Two

(For those fanatics who insist on a fifth line)

I have a dilemma perturbing.
You might even call it disturbing.
Oh, my limericks are rich,
But that fifth line's a bitch!
So, Ya-da-da, Ya-da-da, curbing!

The Hanging Limerick Three

My limericks are quite a disaster,
And sinking me faster and faster.
They sound oh so divine,
'Til I reach the fifth line,
Then…

The Hanging Limerick Four

I told myself I would die trying,
To keep my poor limericks from dying.
After Tai Chi and Zen,
I still botched it again,
And !@#$%^&*()_+)(*&^%o!!!!!

The Hanging Limerick Five

I know this is getting monotonous,
But I need a little more practice,
So I'll try it again,
All the way to the end,
And . . . aw, SHOOT!

The Hanging Limerick Six

I'm glad I'm not really a bettor,
Or one nervous son of a sweater,
For line four's now in debt,
But,
At least my fifth line is much better!

Sixty-Nine

A number that won't be forgotten,
For all the display it has gotten.
I'm a Cancer [69] you see,
On the Zodiac tree,
And what you were thinking is rotten!

Sixty-Nine II

Here's a number you just can't deny,
What you'll have if you're willing to try,
When one's North and one's South,
While attached at the mouth,
And that's not seeing things eye to eye!

Sixty-Nine III

Here's a number you won't soon forget,
For it tells you what you're going to get,
When one's up, and one's down,
While both going to town,
And that's not seeing things tête-à-tête.

The Virgin Juanita

I once met the virgin Juanita,
Back when virgin meant señorita.
She said, "Hell wit romance!
You now pool down yoo pants,
And pleaze me Juanita chiquita!"

Hot Sally Decatur

I once took hot Sally Decatur
Inside an old freight elevator,
Well, we both went to town,
As it bounced up and down,
And baby came down nine months later.

A Lady and a Scamp

A Lady and I went to dinner,
Turns out she was really a sinner.
Well, she calls me a scamp,
And I call her a tramp,
And the next thing I know, I'm in her!

Touchy Feely Harry

Touchy Feely Harry
Now Harry's no Duke to a Duchess,
And never goes far when he touches
A young tender sweet thigh,
But his wife happened by,
And now he walks 'round on his crutches!

Kick the Bucket

I once knew a girl from Nantucket
Who got her ass caught in a bucket.
So she grabbed both her knees,
And with one hearty squeeze,
She farted and managed to chuck it.

The Tenor Maguire

I once heard the tenor Maguire,
When fleeing the scene of a fire,
Slid on slippery wax,
Felt the fireman's axe,
And now he sings one octave higher.

A CANDLE ON FIRE

HODGE PODGE

A CANDLE ON FIRE

Back When

I knew of a place in the Land of OZ,
So I ran down its winding, yellow brick road;
Knew the wonderland of Alice's dream,
And learned of a princess who kissed a toad.
I knew Humpty Dumpty would crack sooner or later,
While Rapunzel struggled to comb her hair.

It wasn't easy raising children in a shoe,
Which a little old woman found more than she could bear.
But these magical lands and these wondrous sights,
Are not what helped me to cope and survive.
Oh, no. It was Dad, the fabler himself, who took me there,
Back when my tale-weaver was still alive.

Die! Witch! Die!

You filthy, miserable witch! Die! Die!
To the depths of hell you psychopath!
And no, don't ever think I'm going to cry.

Vituperatively, you weaved each lie,
With the canine stench of a sociopath,
You filthy, miserable witch!—Die! Die!

Herpetic your womb, and the pus you ply,
So syphilitic, it incurs all wraths;
So no, don't ever think I'm going to cry.

Faced in the gutter you'll be by and by,
In mud you deserve, in blood for a bath,
You miserable, filthy witch! Die! Die!

Those you've stained will come to spit in your eye,
Those unfortunates, who crossed your path;
And no, don't ever think they're going to cry.

And my heart will sing, and my heart will fly,
When they find your corpse in the aftermath!
The filthy, miserable witch, who I begged should die,
And for whom I'm never, ever, going to cry.

Diver Feared Drowned

(Summer of 1975, Orchard Beach)

Suddenly, nobody knows where you are.
The lifeguard, like a seagull, scans the waves from his perch,
And fears the diver may have strayed too far.

The fluid nightmare's surreal, with a twinge of bizarre,
For one moment you're there, like a sinner in church,
Then suddenly, nobody knows where you are.

It is a waiting game, and a rescue repertoire,
The hour long since they began the search,
But it's feared the diver may have strayed too far.

It's hopeless, they whisper, he's gone from the sonar,
Poor wife and daughter, right on the beach, left in the lurch.
It happens, when nobody knows where you are.

But wait! Be it so! Be it the seafaring tar?
There! Like an ocean serpent beneath a watery arch,
Is it the diver, or a buoy that has strayed too far?

From the depths of the Atlantic rises the aquatic star,
And by a daughter's hugs, and many a wifely smooch,
It's certain the diver strayed quite far,
But now, spared by the sea, everyone knows where you are.

In Retrospect

To be untrue to self is to fail self.
Will you place your book on an empty shelf?
Which impostor looks in the mirror and sees
The person who fails in all degrees.

To truly love is to become unquestionable.
To fly high and be truly free is to become irreproachable.
To believe in Truth is to become indestructible.

What then shall I become?

Will I be two or will I be one?
Will I be taken from the shelf?
Or will they take my other self?

I will find out next time I look
Into the glass which holds my book.
And I'll smash myself to bits and see—
Is it him or is it me?

My Paradox

. . . I will never know the true moment of my death,
for once this knowledge is known to me, I will
have altered the course of my future,
and my moment of death becomes
unknown once more; and so,
Death will just have
to wait until I'm
all done
living
. . .
. .
.

Ode to Perseverance

Such patience moves your grace divine,
To carry all from time to time,
(Without a word of discontent)
To save the souls your will has bent.
I've seen your face, I know it well,
Your eyes have lifted mine from hell,
Through steady course, and Eye so keen,
As if by Godness overseen.
I step and fall, then rise and fly,
Because of your unerring eye;
Yet, ask you nothing in return,
Except I walk with you and learn
How to defeat a rocky hill,
Or crush a mountain with my will.

Rhyme at First Hearing

If food for body is a need, my mind
Must have the like to move this frame along.
The eagle needs, beneath its wings, the wind,
To rest upon its breath, and soar among
The clouds, until it need itself to throw
Its frame to earth, in bolting-flash, for food.
Great clouds sharp lightning throw to soothe their brow!
Why not it fly the same for my own good?
I crave the echoed words and sounds which move
My mind to feed my soul, for where I'm from,
The rhyme and I fit one like hand and glove.
It is myself, foremost and first, to whom
I must be true, until, from lack of breath,
My rhymes are ever silenced by my death.

Two Ravens at War

Two lone combatants, in a clear blue sky,
Black Furies from a cold and ancient realm,
Bold Knight against bold Knight, prepare to die,
Head the fall, into the wings of Death's calm.
The dogfight rages against the noon sun,
Ebon ailerons all controlling pitch
And roll, neither giving to be outdone,
Until, Fate steps in, like a bile-filled witch,
And a talon slices the one purblind.
The Icarus-fall commences, to Earth
They drop, fluttering in a deadly grind,
Each aflame, burning for all they are worth!
The ground hits hard, then it prepares for red,
As the nobler beak strikes the other dead.

MY SENTIMENTS EXACTLY

A CANDLE ON FIRE

A Reason for Rhyme

I want my rhymes to weep and sing—
express nostalgia and desire;
thrust fluid verses from the spring
which flood the gates of Dante's fire.

I want to sculpt my words of stone,
so each, when chipped, in fine detail,
may find a soul to spark its own,
and like Rodin's pure art, prevail.

I want to brush my verses faint
with hues from Autumn's falling tears,
and in Monet's own Garden paint
impressions of immortal years.

I want to hear the spraying foam
from where fair Venus rose above,
and from her footprints on the loam
see rise the rhymes of mortal love.

I want to tame my verses wild
the way the cowboy tames his steeds,
then ride into the sunset mild,
with lasso 'round my tumbling weeds.

I want to live in days of old,
when Nymphs and Muses plucked the heart,
and lit the torches brave and bold,
with fire from the rhyming art.

But most of all, I want to teach
all children in the here and now,
that all the forms are theirs to reach,
if masters verse to show them how.

A CANDLE ON FIRE

For every dawn there's end of day,
and like the rest, I'll serve my time.
But rest assured, the world will say:
"The poet gave his life to rhyme."

Though I'm Forgotten

When I am here no more, and gone away,
To where no ink to paper can be penned,
And all my inspirations reach the end,
Remember what, 'til then, I had to say.
Recite my verses, should they suit your day,
And with a stroke, or key, my works amend.
Rewrite — what you see fit — to comprehend,
Or having written well, you bid them stay.
For I will not be there to hold your hand,
Or lead you through the doorways of my mind;
And all I ever was is what you'll find
Inside a poet's only path to fame.
I only hope the world will let them stand,
Though eyes and lips forget — my face, my name.

When My Pen Runs Out of Ink

The day my pen has shed the last of all its tears,
And every drop of ink upon the pages of
My book has dried, denied will not be those who love
The rhyming forms. These echoed words, which bare my years
And life, may be the only proof I lived. My fears
And hopes, which shaped the ink, have driven me, to move
Me to a higher plane of thought, a step above
The normal grind of verse, which never soothed my ears.
So take my verses, written as they are, extol
Them or condemn them, but do something either way.
My death will be your pass to judge them day by day,
Until some night, I hope, they're worth the time you spend
Reciting meager rhymes I had to write, and all
Of which, through diligence and sleepless nights, I penned.

THE END